MW01697474

CHARACTER-DRIVEN, COLLEGE PREPARATION

Parents and Teachers In Partnership Through University-Model Schooling

Dr. John William Turner Jr.

Character Driven

COLLEGE PREPARATION

Parents & Teachers In Partnership Through University-Model Schooling

Dr. John William Turner, Jr.

CHARACTER-DRIVEN, COLLEGE PREPARATION

Parents and Teachers In Partnership Through University-Model Schooling

Table of Contents

DEDICATION

Special funds for this book project were provided by
Jay L. Sedwick, Jr. and Laurie Lovvorn Sedwick
in loving honor of their parents.

But from everlasting to everlasting
the Lord's love is with those who fear him,
and his righteousness with their children's children,
with those who keep his covenant
and remember to obey his precepts.
Psalm 103:17

"This book is dedicated to
Martin & Mary Lovvorn
and
Jay & Linda Sedwick,
with grateful hearts for a godly heritage."

SPECIAL THANKS

Any book is not the author's alone. It is the product of countless people who have influenced and supported him. This is especially true here.

First, both the author and his wife are indebted to their own parents—John & Mozelle Turner and Garland & Dorothy Jo Osborn—for being the involved and loving parents that they were and are.

Second, the author is forever indebted to his beloved wife Roxie. Her remarkable effectiveness as a teaching parent and her sacrificial support for this specific project are the reason why he would ever have the opportunity to write on the subject at hand.

Third, the author is deeply grateful to the five children that he and Roxie are so very blessed to parent. Mandi, Ginger, John, Thomas, and Bekah, though fully "human," continually choose to live in such a way that when their parents speak about the teaching of children, others want to listen. That is a precious gift of God!

Finally, the author offers his heartfelt thanks to the entire University-Model Schooling community who, through honest hard work and cooperative commitment, have pioneered a fresh, wise, and practical approach to pre-college education in America. In keeping with their character, many have preferred not to be named here, but let the reader understand: *they are the real authors of this book!*

Thank you all.

CHAPTER

1 How We Discovered University-Model Schooling

I'm not a salesman for University-Model Schooling (UMS). I'm a satisfied customer.

Putting myself in your place, I can imagine scanning this page right now and wondering, "Who is this guy, and what in the world is he doing here?"

I'll try to answer that in this chapter.

Then, it will be my privilege to introduce you to a new model of college-preparatory education (UMS) that is incredibly effective *for the elementary through high-school grades.* In UMS, students take challenging, age-appropriate courses of study that are set in *a university-type scheduling of classes* — either on Monday-Wednesday-Friday or Tuesday-Thursday. Outside of class, the students work to develop *sound study habits* and the kind of *strong work ethic* they will need for success in college. This is assured because of the attention paid to an essential ingredient that the U.S. Department of Education repeatedly affirms as a proven difference-maker in any child's education: *meaningful and wise parental mentoring.* How it all works will be explained in the chapters that follow, but first I would like you to know that, for me, UMS is not just an intriguing theory. It is a personal experience. I am a father of UMS students.

The groundwork for my appreciation of UMS was laid in my own upbringing. I can illustrate by showing you a couple of snapshots from my childhood. I just happen to have them with me, right here in the wallet of my memory banks. Would you like to "see" them?

This is my Mom, and that's me when I was six years old. If you look closely, you can see that she is holding some of my schoolbooks — the English ones. We were citizens of the USA living overseas in an Arabic-speaking country. Every weekday afternoon when I got home from my Arabic first-grade class, Mom would take me through some additional lessons in English. This picture was taken just seconds after Mom asked me, "John, would you like to sit down now and do this reading with me?"

I answered, "No thanks, Mom, that's alright. You go right ahead."

She loved telling that story to people.

This next picture here is of my Dad. That's one of my sisters there with him. If I saw this scene once, I'll bet I saw it a thousand times: Dad sitting down to help at least one of us with homework. All five of us kids could tell you stories about Dad somehow pulling us through a tough, last-minute study situation in the "nick of time."

That serious look on Dad's face is because he is trying to figure things out for himself before teaching my sister. For me, that was always a good time to go get a sandwich.

You know what? Those sessions with Mom and Dad taught us *much more* than lessons from books. We couldn't help but also learn about love, care, priorities, and sacrifice. Just by being with them, we got an education in living, laughing, cheering, and crying — *together.*

We adopted not only their values but their faith as well. We *wanted* to know the loving God they knew, who delights in giving good gifts to His children.

Oh! Speaking of children and gifts: the last picture I want to show you is on the very next page. *Our* five children surprised Roxie and me with this picture of themselves on our twenty-fifth wedding anniversary. Meet our children, Mandi, Ginger, John, Thomas, and Bekah.

What a thrill it is to take the legacy of love we have received and pass it to the next generation — even to the generations we will never see! Is there anything greater than that?

University-Model schools give parents more time for being with their children than do traditional schools. This gives parents greater opportunity to impart the faith and values they hold precious. Students from public, private, and home schools alike are being attracted to the model because of its uniquely *balanced approach* to partnering with parents and preparing students.

Would you like to know how *we* discovered University-Model Schooling? Remember, we are just one family with one story. Families have entered the UMS community from a variety of public as well as private school backgrounds. The reason I share our experience here is to illustrate some of the unique benefits and flexibility of the model. I hope that the picture this paints in your mind will be helpful when you study the more technical descriptions of UMS later in this book.

Our Story

In the spring of 1993, we were settling into a new home after moving halfway across the country. Here was the situation: Mandi was approaching tenth grade; Ginger, eighth; John, fifth; Thomas, second; and Bekah was not yet two years old. Until that time, we had taught all of them at home. I did my best to help; but, of course, it was Roxie who carried the day-to-day load of responsibility. And she loved every minute of it!

To say that Roxie had done a tremendous job would grossly *under*state the high quality of her work as a wife, mother, mentor, and teacher. She was (and is) amazing! Her first priority was home, yet she still carried on various ministries with people outside our home.

For Roxie, teaching our kids was more than a preference and more than a studied conclusion as to what method of educating was best. It was a *calling*, an integral part of her God-given identity and mission in life. Since I was the one blessed to be her husband, that made me part of that calling, too. For that, I can never thank God enough. What an astounding difference that *shared calling* has made in our children's lives and in our family!

In 1993, our calling to teach our kids was as clear as ever, but our ways of living out the calling began to change.

That spring, you might say we went through a kind of "storm before the calm." The storm was not terrible, but threatening nonetheless. Both Roxie and I could see the clouds coming from a distance, but each of our responses was different. Roxie took the matter seriously yet was sure we would weather the storm just fine. I guess I was the one that panicked when I saw this huge wall of mystery approaching called "Mandi's TENTH grade." Whoa, scary!

That meant she had only three more years until . . . *COLLEGE!* Were *we* ready to get *her* ready?

I saw that dark, ominous thing coming and wanted to run for cover! I started checking out every "storm shelter" around — every local school option I could think of. Some of the ideas I came up with in those days startled Roxie more than the storm itself! Was I abandoning our call, she wondered? I did not *think* so. But did that big storm cloud scare me?

Do I *have* to admit that I think it did?

Roxie was totally calm and confident but agreed that together we should search for additional resources and/or tutors to assist with the college-preparatory math and science courses that we knew Mandi needed. We considered many possibilities, but in light of the calling we understood and the busy schedules we kept, none of the options fit.

The rest of the story is the reason I am writing this book.

In May of that year, Roxie and I attended a huge convention on education held annually in our city. We were still on our quest for "shelter" as we attended seminars and browsed displays of curricula and resources. At the end of the day, with our arms full of books and brochures, we were tired and ready to go home to process. As we headed for the parking lot, I suddenly remembered one more resource that I wanted to check out. Roxie waited as I hurried back into the convention hall.

I do not remember what the resource was. All I remember was that, when I finished conversing with the spokesperson about his display, he said something in passing about a new school getting under way in our city. *It was a different kind of academy that required less time in classrooms and more time at home in order to provide an effective transition to college.* I was in a hurry, so I said something like, "Uh huh, well, thank you very much," then turned to go.

The next thing I did, could have looked like one of those double takes in an old TV sitcom. I walked three steps away from the man, halted dead in my tracks with a wide-eyed stare, then slowly turned back to the man and asked, "What was that you just said?"

I cocked my head slightly to listen so that, as he repeated each word, at least one ear would be likely to get it right! When I was sure that I had heard him correctly, I scribbled down the phone number for more information, went home, and called as soon as I could.

The more Roxie and I learned about this new academy, the more intrigued we became. We agreed that we should start the application process so that we could at least ask more questions. Every step in the process led us to greater agreement that this was an alternative worth trying. We had never heard of a school like this before! It offered the college-preparatory assistance we needed in a way that was both consistent with and supportive of our desire to continue investing in our children at home. We now know that the academy was the *first* to test University-Model Schooling (UMS) as it is described in this book.

We enrolled both Mandi and Ginger that fall. Our roles with them then shifted from being *primary* teachers to that of *partner*-teachers with each of their excellent, professional instructors. Qualified, dedicated adults presented academic material to Mandi and Ginger in classes that met three hours a week (like a college class) while we accepted responsibility for giving them additional guidance at home, keeping them on track in their academically challenging curriculum. (See Chapter 5 for more on the various roles that parents play in the learning design of a University-Model school.)

Meanwhile, Roxie continued her full-time work with John, Thomas, and Bekah at home. Over the next three years, John was able to take a few courses at the University-Model school in math and art; then he began a full load of courses his eighth-grade year. Attending class primarily on Monday, Wednesday, and Friday, he then studied on Tuesday, Thursday, and Saturday under our guidance at home. Similarly, Thomas began easing into the curriculum in the seventh grade and began his full load in the ninth. Bekah, who at this writing is approaching fourth grade, is still being taught at home.

Update and Summary

How effective was this model in preparing Mandi and Ginger for college? Well, Ginger began her junior year in college with a GPA of 3.9. Mandi graduated *summa cum laude* in May 2000, and began her training to become a medical doctor the following August at the University of Texas Medical Branch in Galveston, Texas. The delight of our hearts, however, is that each of them has a confident, vibrant faith and a wholesome mission and direction in life. We attribute all of this to the marvelous grace of God and the wisdom of His ways.

How is the University-Model "test school" doing? While controlling growth each year, it has grown from its original 186 students to over 500 in eight years. Hundreds more are on a waiting list to be admitted while the majority of those graduating receive college scholarship offers. Some students, like ours, transition into the academy from home schools. Others come into the University Model from full-time public or private schools. By now, there is also a growing population of students who started elementary school at the UMS test school and plan to continue all the way through graduation from high school.

Some students at the test school take only one or two classes a semester and receive the rest of their instruction at home. Others take a full load of five or six courses a semester and will graduate with a diploma that is commanding greater and greater respect among the nation's universities because of the college-simulated training it represents.

Some families are drawn to the model because, compared to traditional schools, it offers *greater access for parents to stay involved* in the most important dimension of their children's education — their values and character formation. Others are interested in the high academic standards and strong work ethic promoted through the *college-simulated learning environment*, which successfully eases the transition into higher education. Still others are attracted to the *character emphasis* built into every aspect of the school's service, including the academic and student activities programs.

Whether coming from public, private, or home schools, all families are admitted into University-Model Schooling with the understanding that a high degree of parental mentoring will be expected. While it is true that all approaches to education are strengthened when parents are meaningfully involved, the University Model absolutely depends upon it. Without someone who will provide responsible parenting, it is difficult to imagine how the model could ever work.

The University-Model approach is certainly not to be considered the *only* way or the "right" way for everyone. Every family faces different circumstances; therefore, each has a different set of needs. To believe that one educational alternative is right for every family is to believe that every situation is the same. This, of course, is not the case.

It is our hope that ALL parents reading these pages will be challenged by the principles that undergird the University Model and find renewed courage and confidence to accept their unique roles in their children's educational journeys. We desire to see parents inspired to seize the extraordinary opportunities they have to make a positive difference in the next generation. If this book motivates even a few passive, timid, or discouraged parents to think, take heart, and become more positively active in their children's educational lives, then this work will be a success.

CHAPTER

2 It's Time to Contribute, Not Complain

Far too many families are poorly served by our chaotic, unresponsive, and inequitable educational system. Pervasively low test scores and high dropout rates, which in many cities approach 50 percent, degrade our workforce and signal a staggering waste of human potential. The urgent national reports that have chronicled these disorders in detail indeed present a picture of a nation at risk. If we are to be judged by how we treat our children, we face stern treatment.[1]

The crisis in American education is well-documented. This book is *not* an attempt to analyze the complexities of the crisis itself. It attempts instead to address some critical needs in a positive way — to contribute rather than complain, to share responsibility rather than assign blame.

This presentation of University-Model Schooling for the elementary through high school grades is supported by seven years of practical experience and verifiable results. It makes no claim to have *the* "final answer" for every million-dollar question, but it offers a compelling idea that is edu-

[1] Anne T. Henderson and Nancy Berla, eds., *A New Generation of Evidence: The Family Is Critical to Student Achievement* (Washington, D.C.: National Committee for Citizens in Education, 1994), 19.

cationally solid, logistically practical, and fiscally efficient. Its worthiness of serious consideration in a variety of educational settings is earned.

Good and Smart

Developmental psychologist Thomas Lickona observed, "Down through history, education has had two great goals: to help people become smart and to help people become good."[2] His statement is a reminder that genuine education is a healthy blend of both mental and moral instruction. Teaching, therefore, is more than just organizing and presenting lessons. It is also *defining* what is and is not acceptable classroom behavior, *enforcing* order through appropriate rewards and punishments, and *motivating* students to want and work for that which is best for themselves and for others. These classroom management functions cannot be accomplished apart from clearly communicated directives that appeal to students' hearts as well as their minds. For this reason, it is impossible to separate good academic instruction from some form of moral training as well. Helping students become "smart," then, must also incorporate efforts to help them become "good," otherwise students may become neither.

Effective teachers are keenly aware of these values-based dimensions of their craft. They also understand that knowing what to do *in theory* and doing it successfully *in practice* are two entirely different matters. One reason is that there is yet another variable in the teaching equation that, for many, is increasingly difficult to solve: *cooperative students.*

Even in the early 1990s, syndicated columnist and author William Murchison summarized a social scene that has become all too graphically familiar to the American public in recent years:

> We have noted already the violence that shakes and sunders many school campuses — attacks on teachers by students, attacks on stu-

[2] Thomas Lickona, "The Return of Character Education" (*Education Leadership*, vol. 51, no. 3, November 1993), 6.

> dents by other students, murders by students or outsiders. This is awful — and yet it is not even the whole woeful picture. American young people are victims and exemplars of a broad decline in moral standards. Two out of three teenage drinkers begin in the ninth grade. Suicide, once a rarity among teenagers, now is the third most common cause of death in that age bracket, after accidents and murders. Unwanted pregnancies in the mid-1980s rose 23 percent among children ten to fourteen years of age; among the same age group, gonorrhea quadrupled between 1960 and 1988. According to a survey in 1993, nine out of ten high-school students say cheating takes place in their schools; three out of four say students steal from each other.
>
> This audience undoubtedly is ripe for moral instruction. Whether the setting is right and the means are right are separate questions. But that schools can do *something* is plain.[3]

Indeed, schools *must* "do something" to address basic moral concerns or academic achievement will continue to suffer as well. But can schools take on these issues alone?

Sharing Responsibility

To lay the responsibility for America's educational crisis *only* on the schools is to fail to understand the issues. The social dynamics that schools experience are best viewed as symptomatic of a complex mixture of other societal ills. For example, even in the best of school situations, teachers and administrators must work with children who are products of home environments that both precede them and extend beyond their scopes of supervision. Parents are the ones responsible for preparing their children to show, at the very least, reasonable respect for authority and basic consideration of others so that, once in school, their instruction can be accomplished in

[3] William Murchison, *Reclaiming Morality in America* (Nashville: Thomas Nelson, 1994), 145-46.

an ordered environment conducive to learning. Teachers have no choice but to work with what is given (or not given) them by the parents.

Those same parents, however, have their own personal problems to overcome, marriages to hold together (or recover from), livings to make, expenses to pay, and "lifestyles" to pursue — all in the midst of a culture of rapid change, relative values, and media illusions. Children and their needs, including their proper training, are easily lost in the milieu.

Children Are Stressed

David Elkind, professor of child study at Tufts University, has concluded that in today's postmodern culture, children and youth are under even greater stress than adults. In his book *Ties That Stress*, he asserts that, whereas there used to be major focus on understanding the developmental needs of children, now there is more emphasis on the "passages" and needs of adults. Whereas children used to be allowed a wide variety of mistakes in judgment as a part of growing up and learning, now they are more quickly labeled as deviant, even criminal, while adults are permitted the broader range of "acceptable" behaviors. And whereas children used to have plenty of wide-open spaces available to them for safe exploration and play, now adults occupy those spaces and children must limit their options to be protected. Elkind summarizes these observations by sadly concluding:

> When young people's developmental needs for protection and nurture are ignored, when their human differences in growth rates and behavior are deemed deviant, and when they are given little or no space to live and to grow, they are stressed. Young people who are stressed often do what adults do: they engage in actions that are destructive to themselves, to others, or to both. The consequences of these self/other punishing practices are increasingly evident.[4]

[4] David Elkind, *Ties That Stress* (Harvard University Press, 1994), 188-89.

If Elkind is even close to being correct, then it follows that schools inherit the results, first of all, of a culture that gives myriad lifestyle choices to adults while providing less and less space and priority for children. This makes it easy for parents to get caught up in a fast-paced world of multiple obligations, confused values, and time limitations. Regularly on the lookout for the next convenient way to get the kids taken care of, they busy themselves with other "needs." Their children, on the other hand, are expected to become competent, responsible "little adults" in a world of temporary relationships and changing rules.

But that is just the beginning of what teachers and school administrators inherit from American culture. Violent and sexually oriented media are more graphic and accessible than ever before. Weapons and drugs are easily obtained. The intimate details of crime, deceit, sexual immorality, exploitation, and abuse are discussed as public information while ultimate values and morality are dismissed as private concerns. Educators are often left with the burden of coping in school with effects that result from causes they cannot fully remedy.

Schools Are Us!

All of these factors affect the learning environment. They impact teaching profoundly, though teachers can influence them little. If parents or politicians ever try to lay the nation's educational problems *solely* at the feet of America's schools, then a proper retort might be a paraphrase of Pogo's classic comic line: "We have met the schools and the schools are us!"

Schools reflect homes. Research validates that when homes are strengthened, schools improve. University-Model schools are successfully accessing the most powerful known single influence for reforming education in America: meaningfully involved parents!

Teachers, wherever they serve, are to be saluted for their efforts to educate students and make a difference in the world. Schools, whether public or private, deserve community and especially parental support. Effective education that helps people become both smart and good is a task bigger and more complicated than school alone. It is a community responsibility that begins in the home, and then extends to every sector of community life — religious, legal, governmental, social, and scholastic.

University-Model schools wish to demonstrate a healthy, successful educational alternative in an attitude of partnership with the larger community of local leaders and educators. While the model has much to offer pre-college students of all ages, it is also understood that every local community needs to have a variety of viable educational choices available in order to meet the diverse needs of today's families. UMS proponents believe that their chosen educational paradigm will contribute significantly to the ongoing dialogue that seeks to improve education in America.

CHAPTER

3 The "A-Parent" Needs of Every Student

The evidence is now beyond dispute. When schools work together with families to support learning, children tend to succeed not just in school, but also throughout life. In fact, the most accurate predictor of a student's achievement in school is not income or social status, but the extent to which that student's family is able to:

1. *Create a home environment that encourages learning.*
2. *Express high (but not unrealistic) expectations for their children's achievement and future careers.*
3. *Become involved in their children's education at school and in the community.*[5]

Parents teach. They teach by what they do. They teach by what they say. They teach by how they live and make decisions.

The proponents of University-Model Schooling wish to applaud all

[5] Henderson, 1.

parents who take their roles as mentors and educators seriously and conscientiously. Such parents provide their children with the most strategic educational advantage available — themselves.

Parents teach many things on purpose, while imparting a host of other things unintentionally. Delighted is the parent who makes the happy discovery that a child has learned a positive trait simply by imitating Mom or Dad. Disappointed, even despairing, can be the parent who sadly awakens to the realization that a child is reflecting a negative trait first learned at the hands of *you know who*. Yes, it may be good news or bad, but the fact remains: parents teach.

Because parents are their kids' first teachers, they have no choice but to travel a journey with them called *education*. Many intriguing pathways of learning will be offered for them to consider along the way, but the option of staying in one place — that is, of not making the trip — is unavailable. Parents go with their children on the education journey whether accepting or denying, willing or unwilling, active or passive. And just as some parents' most important teaching may be unintentional, naturally flowing out of who they are, so some of their most critical educational decisions may be uninformed, naively based in the assumption that what is "best" for the parents must also be best for the child. *Wise parents realize that, in addition to being their children's first teachers, they are also the primary guides of the process that allows additional teachers to enter and influence their children's worlds.* Parents who understand this and prioritize the children's needs over their own, dedicating personal time and energy for positive involvement in their children's education, will enjoy satisfying long-term dividends.

Parents Teach As Parents Are

One of the biggest mistakes a parent can make is to equate sending kids to school with giving them an education. Schooling is in fact only one of the primary colors in the total spectrum of a child's education. There are indeed some formal aspects of education that schools can address; but the broader and more critical aspects of education are administered by a child's parents. This remains true even if some parents wish it to be otherwise.

By the very nature of who they are, parents regularly present a body of instruction to their children called *beliefs and values*. Whether positive or negative, constructive or destructive, these beliefs and values are caught and taught in the informal arena of everyday life. Through their attitudes, actions, direct instructions as well as casual conversations, parents impart priorities and a way of life — a framework within which their children will organize the experiences and information from their early years.

Once children are attending school, they need their parents *more*, not less. Josh McDowell and Bob Hostetler, active observers of today's culture, comment:

> Parents have changed their thinking; these days, parents expect professionals to educate their children. If I were to ask a group of 100 parents, 'Who is in charge of your child's education?' I would expect the majority of them to answer 'Mrs. Johnson,' 'Mr. Philips,' or 'St. Ursula School.' Few of them would answer, 'Me.' The most important change in education in the last fifty years has not occurred in schools; it has occurred in the minds of parents, who no longer take responsibility for their children's educations.[6]

Harry and Rosemary Wong, long-time educators who have written several books on improving teacher effectiveness, emphasize the importance of showing love to students by noting:

- The average child receives 12 minutes of attention each day from his or her parents.
- The average parent watches five to six hours of television each day.
- The number one problem reported by high school students is loneliness.

[6] Josh McDowell & Bob Hostetler, *Right From Wrong: What You Need to Know to Help Youth Make Right Choices* (Dallas: Word Publishing, 1994), 41.

The Carnegie Foundation surveyed 22,000 teachers.

- 90 percent said that a lack of parental support was a problem at their schools. . . .
- 100 percent described their students as 'emotionally needy and starved for attention and affection.'[7]

Parents' educational responsibilities do not end when they place their children in school. On the contrary, there is the real sense in which, once the kids are in school, the parents' task of educating has only begun. School — any school beyond the home itself — intensifies the influences of a host of competing values with which a child must learn to contend. It is not the time for parents to move on to other concerns in the illusion that the kids' educational needs are now met. Instead, it is time for them to fully engage their most vigilant involvement, concentrated energy, and creative instruction for a course called *character formation*. Sons and daughters need to be taught how to live for a purpose larger than themselves (faith in and love for God), how to distinguish right from wrong (truth and morality), how to incorporate positive values into their lives (knowledge and discipline), and how to stand courageously against the negative values that bring harm to themselves and others (brotherly love and community). To do so requires the strategic use of *time*, that commodity which ever escapes until parents intentionally capture and employ it.

But Do I Get An "A"?

The influence of parents, however, extends far beyond the priority concerns of values and character. It reaches all the way to the practical, down-to-earth, raw results of good grades and college-worthy academic

[7] Harry K. Wong & Rosemary T. Wong, *The First Days of School: How To Be An Effective Teacher* (Mountain View, CA: Harry K. Wong Publications, 1998), 76.

performance. Time and again, careful research has demonstrated that what parents do (or do *not* do) greatly impacts student academic performance. In 1994, the U.S. Department of Education indicated that "controllable home factors account for almost all the differences in average student achievement across states."[8] Parents who assume that schools function fine without them are sadly mistaken.

Publications of the Department of Education often repeat summaries like the following, which is taken from a 1997 "Idea Book" entitled, *Family Involvement In Children's Education*:

> Thirty years of research confirms that family involvement is a powerful influence on children's achievement in school. . . . When families are involved in their children's education, children earn higher grades and receive higher scores on tests, attend school more regularly, complete more homework, demonstrate more positive attitudes and behaviors, graduate from high school at higher rates, and are more likely to enroll in higher education than students with less involved families. For these reasons, increasing family involvement in the education of their children is an important goal for schools, particularly those serving low-income and other students at risk of failure.[9]

The Department of Education uses the term "family involvement" because of the reality that some parents are either absent or otherwise unable to help their children, in which case a grandparent, uncle, aunt, or other "loved one" must fill the gap. In addressing such situations, many researchers agree with Thomas Kellaghan and his team who conclude,

---

[8] U.S. Department of Education, "Strong Families, Strong Schools: Building Community Partnerships For Learning" (Washington, D.C.: U.S. Government Printing Office, September 1994).

[9] *Family Involvement in Children's Education* (U.S. Department of Education, http://www.ed.gov/pubs/FamInvolve/execsumm.html, 1997), Executive Summary, 1.

> Today, many commentators would view any attempt at intervention with children from disadvantaged backgrounds that did not include a home component as unlikely to be very effective.[10]

Without a doubt, good teachers are essential to good education. The above studies, however, raise the honest question, "How many good teachers have been less highly esteemed than they should have been — not because their skills were deficient, but because they lacked the most influential factor that contributes to their full effectiveness: parental support?"

For parents, the commitment to be involved translates into the making of deliberate, often difficult, scheduling decisions that keep them moving *toward* the children and their educational needs. Parents who schedule too many things *away* from the children, thinking that now there is a school to "teach" them, are shortsighted. They may later be forced to make more drastic adjustments around a child who has succumbed to a competing value like "partying" and is now dealing with declining grades, a drug dependency, a pregnancy, or worse — heartbreaking consequences that might have been prevented had the parents more assertively positioned themselves in their rightful places as involved, vigilant, creative, and loving educators.

■ Parents Need Encouragement

Schools are poor substitutes for parents. Without parental support, schools are like buildings lacking a foundation. More time must be dedicated to preventing collapse than to purposeful use. Indeed, many of today's teachers are forced to spend more time addressing unmet parenting needs than unlearned academic material. In some schools, keeping order alone can be deemed a major accomplishment.

Unfortunately, many of the proposed "solutions" to America's educational problems actually recommend more time in class, removing students

---

[10] Thomas, Kellaghan, et al., *The Home Environment and School Learning: Promoting Parental Involvement in the Education of Children* (1993), 13.

even further from the teachers most needed in the process: parents! Why not look for ways to encourage and lift the confidence levels of today's stressed and overwhelmed parent-educators? Why not assume that, given the right opportunity and tools, many parents will favorably respond?

Henderson and Berla, who in 1994 co-edited one of the most often quoted reviews of the research on families in education (and often quoted in this book as well), affirm,

> When they are treated as partners and given good information by people with whom they are comfortable, parents put into practice the strategies they already know are effective, but have not had the confidence or experience yet to attempt.[11]

University-Model schools are not only empowering and "employing" parents in their teaching paradigm, they are also demonstrating the positive difference made when parents know that they are built into the learning process — needed, wanted, and expected.

It is true that there are some families today for whom the University Model is simply not an option. If there is not an available parent or acting parent (grandparent, foster parent, etc.) in a child's life capable of participating in the model, then, of course, other alternatives may be necessary and should be sought.

For most families, however, the question is not one of parental capability or availability. It is a question of willingness to adjust priority time toward the children and their needs. For the parent who wonders, "Can I do it?" there are many supports and encouragements built into the University-Model program design.

It may help now to see the bigger picture of University-Model Schooling before looking at the specific roles that parents play in the UMS learning design.

---

[11] Henderson, 11.

CHAPTER

4 Essential Elements in the University Model

Involving parents will not compensate for an inadequate reading program, any more than public relations campaigns will cover up poor instruction and low expectations. Collaboration with families is an essential component of a reform strategy, but it is not a substitute for a high quality education program or thoughtful, comprehensive school improvement.[12]

■ What is University-Model Schooling?

University-Model Schooling (UMS) is a new educational alternative that, until now, has not been among the typical choices available to parents. Though off-campus parental roles are clearly defined and required in the model, UMS should *not* be equated with home schooling or home schooling cooperatives. Nor should UMS be understood as traditional classroom education that has simply reduced classroom time. Its significance lies in its ability to effectively utilize parents in partnership with highly

[12] Henderson, 13.

qualified professional instructors to gain better academic results, especially among average students. This partnership is facilitated by using a university-type schedule, administrative system, and strong work ethic in age-appropriate ways for the elementary through high school grades. The result is an excellent, well-rounded education with less time in school, less cost for families, increased opportunities for positive parent-child interaction, and improved order and discipline in the classroom. It also results in the successful transition of students directly into college with minimal "culture shock" since they have already experienced a college-simulated work environment at the high school level.

UMS is designed to bring together the best attributes of traditional schooling with the best attributes of home schooling and integrate them into one model. The immediate goal is quality, cost-effective, college-preparatory education accomplished in a way that gives parents more time for imparting the faith and values they hold precious. The ultimate goal is that of producing wholesome, competent men and women of character who make a positive difference in the next generation. It is also hoped that University-Model schools, both public and private, can gain nationwide acceptance among parents and educators as a schooling alternative that is needed in every community.

A quick look at where University-Model Schooling stands in relation to existing educational alternatives is visualized in Figures 1 and 2 on the following pages.

Comparing Schools by Their Levels of Required Parental Involvement

Degrees of Parental Involvement ***Required*** *in American Schools*

Boarding/State Schools	Traditional Schools	University-Model Schools	Home Schools
Public Private	**Public Private**	**Public Private**	**Private**

Fig. 1

This diagram looks at various educational alternatives from the viewpoint of ***the involvement level required of parents*** in the process, a factor that for decades has been considered vital in the overall success of students, both academically and socially. Charter schools could also be added to each category diagrammed above except for home schooling.

The University-Model Schooling Gradual Transition Into College

Figure 2 illustrates the gradual transition into college that University-Model Schooling provides. In traditional classroom schooling, students spend from 35 to 40 hours in class each week. In college, however, they will only be in class from 15 to 20 hours each week and need to discipline themselves to use the remaining time for study. For many students, this is a difficult transition, and it requires the first year of college just to get adjusted. By the time a University-Model student is in high school, he or she will already be experiencing a simulated college environment and developing the necessary disciplines and skills for succeeding in that environment. Previously home-schooled students have different kinds of adjustments to make, depending upon their experience. University- Model Schooling also provides them with an excellent, natural transition into a college environment.

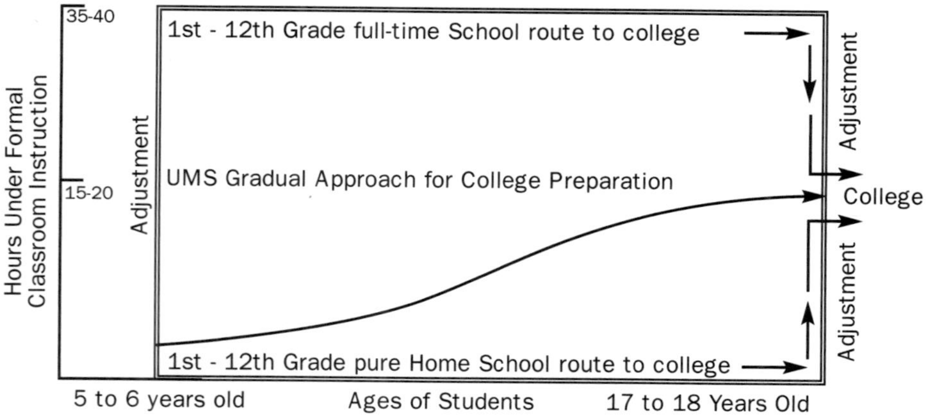

Fig. 2

The Three-Program Design of a University-Model School

A fully developed University-Model school consists of three interdependent, educational programs. They are the Academic, Character Development, and Student Activities programs. All three work in support of and in dependence upon each other for their optimum effectiveness. *Each program utilizes an integrated approach involving both the professional instructor at school and the willing parent at home.* To coordinate the interdependent work of the three programs, it is also necessary to provide centralized Program Support functions, including administrative, business, and property management. The three programs in the UMS model along with their support functions are illustrated in figure 3.

Representation of a fully developed University Model School

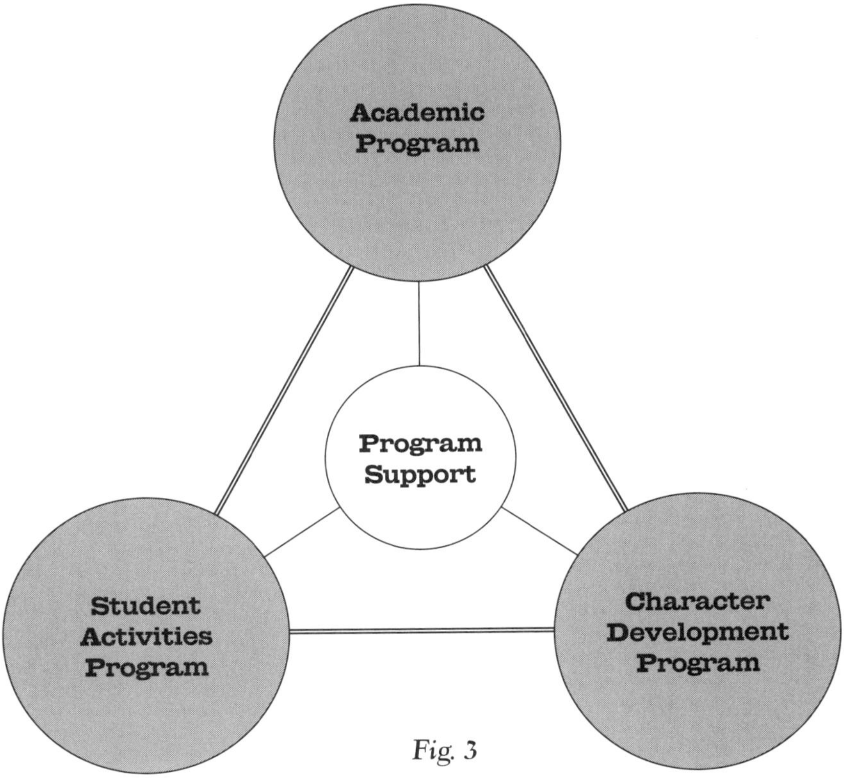

Fig. 3

The three-program design of a University-Model school can be applied in both public and private school settings. In the public system, it would seem to work best as an alternative charter school, emphasizing specific character goals for students along with the necessary family-involvement dynamics. In a private school setting, the character emphasis can be explicitly faith-based as well.

The original University-Model test school referred to in Chapter 1 was organized as a private Christian school. Most of the information that follows, therefore, results from experience gained there. An attempt is made, however, to communicate the basic design in such a way that it can be implemented anywhere.

Since UMS can be useful in a variety of situations, many methodological decisions are school-specific. Little effort is made in this section to explore those variables but rather to present the larger view. Seminars are available for educators who desire in-depth orientation to the working details of the model as well as to the specific methods chosen by the test school. Contact information is provided on page 63 at the end of this book.

For the Academic, Character Development, and Student Activities programs to work together effectively, there are necessary elements for each that are highlighted in **bold** letters below. Special required features of each element appear in *italics.*

■ The Academic Program

The Academic Program oversees the entire system of courses, teaching personnel, and standards patterned in many ways after a typical university. This begins with the necessary element of **a college-simulated scheduling of courses**, organized in *16- to 18-week semesters*, with most classes meeting three hours a week — either for one hour on Monday, Wednesday, and Friday (MWF) or for one and one-half hours on Tuesday and Thursday (TTh). This allows for the possibility of the multiple use of space on alternate days resulting in significant cost savings to families.

As students progress into high school, they are encouraged to begin taking courses on both TTh and MWF, much like they will soon do in college. This especially helps high school seniors in two ways: it keeps them from having too many upper-level courses in one day (potentially as many as six), and it gives them experience with the kind of schedule they will be responsible for managing the following year as freshmen in college. The UMS test school, for example, offers the upper-level courses of Calculus I and II, Physics, Chemistry, Anatomy & Physiology, Spanish III and IV, Senior English, Computer II, and Government/Economics/Philosophy. As in college, UMS juniors and seniors are encouraged to take no more than four of these courses on a given day for optimum learning potential.

All academic classes in a University-Model school must be offered as single subject and single grade-level classes in order to best utilize available instructional time. Combining subjects or grade levels within the same class, as many private and small public schools do, is not academically acceptable for a University-Model school. Among the basic high school subjects offered at the UMS test school are English, Computers, Foreign Languages, Math, Science, and Social Studies along with a fine arts program that includes Creative Writing, Art, Choir, Drama, Photography, and Fine Arts Appreciation. Both an honors and standard-level program are available.

Course prerequisites must also be established to provide teachers with a clear starting point for each semester's instruction. Since class time moves rapidly, it is important that students share a similar level of knowledge at the beginning of the course. Once a semester is under way, new students may not be admitted until the beginning of a new semester so that classes can make maximum progress. *Semester-by-semester registration*, therefore, is required.

Even at the elementary level, *course registration in a University-Model school must be flexible enough for students to advance by individual course rather than by complete grade level.* This ensures mastery of all subject matter in a given area of study. Flexibility in course registration makes it possible for students to advance more quickly in areas where they are gifted and/or repeat weaker areas when necessary. This flexibility, however, makes careful diploma planning essential.

Continuity of instruction is assured through *well-developed and clearly articulated curriculum documents*, another requirement of a University-Model school. This is a need not only within a given sequence of courses but also between the central institution and the home.

Critically important to understand is that on days that the students are not in class, they are still "in school" under the tutelage and/or supervision of a parent. This leads to the second necessary element of the Academic Program: **integrated instructional models**. A University-Model school must use instructional designs that effectively integrate the educational responsibilities of parents with those of teachers. Among other things, this means that *each course at each grade level must have a defined and appropriate off-campus role for parents* that gradually decreases their academic (direct teaching) responsibilities while increasing those of the student (dependent and independent study) as he or she progresses through the grade levels. It also means that *effective methods of teacher-parent communication* be utilized. The specific roles that parents play at the different stages of their children's development are explained in the next chapter.

Another vital element in a UMS Academic Program is **teachers who are able to organize instruction that includes parents as off-campus partners**. Teachers must be able to participate in the integrated instructional approach that involves parents. For many teachers this is a dream situation since every student in their classes has an actively supportive parent at home ready and willing to help. Not only must teachers be positive character role models, they must also demonstrate personal mastery over the course content they teach, the skills to communicate that content effectively, and the ability to motivate and inspire students toward learning.

The partnership between parents and professional teachers makes yet another element essential, that of **educational materials that are both**

academically sound and parent/student friendly. Since parents play a vital instructional role with their children, materials need to be easy to use (especially in the younger grades when more parental tutoring is involved) as well as academically solid for all grade levels.

Two other critical elements of the Academic Program are (1) **high academic standards emphasizing a strong student work ethic** and (2) **low student/teacher ratio**. Educators understand the correlation between these two important factors. Although less time is spent in the formal classroom, a UMS academic program is still a very challenging full-time program. High, college-preparatory standards must be set to encourage the development and maintenance of a strong work ethic. The low student/teacher ratios provide for more effective teaching and thus better use of limited classroom time. They also encourage stronger accountability for maintaining the student work ethic. In the UMS test school, the student/teacher ratio limits are set at 16:1 for elementary grades, 18:1 for junior high, and 20:1 for senior high.

Finally, a UMS Academic Program must **meet or exceed the local and state laws that govern education**. Since these laws vary from state to state and community to community, it is understood that each of the basic elements and features indicated above shall be implemented in a manner consistent with and not contrary to the area's governmental guidelines.

■ Review of the Academic Program

- **A College-Simulated Scheduling of Courses**
  - *Sixteen- to Eighteen-Week Semesters*
  - *Single Subject and Single Grade-Level Classes*
  - *Course Prerequisites*
  - *Semester-By-Semester Registration*
  - *Flexibility in Course Registration*
  - *Well-Developed and Clearly-Articulated Curriculum Documents*

- Integrated (Parent-Professional) Instructional Models
  - *Defined, Grade-Level Appropriate, Off-Campus Roles for Parents*
  - *Effective Methods of Teacher-Parent Communication*
- Teachers Able to Organize Instruction That Includes Parents
- Educational Materials That Are Both Academically Sound and Parent/Student Friendly
- High Academic Standards Emphasizing a Strong Student Work Ethic
- Low Student/Teacher Ratio
- Standards That Meet or Exceed the Local and State Laws That Govern Education

The Character Development Program

The Character Development Program oversees the systems set in place to (1) keep parents confident, competent, encouraged, and involved with their children; (2) reinforce values that the parents are on record as teaching in the home; and (3) enforce the behavior and discipline policies of the school from a character development point of view.

The first necessary element in the Character Development Program is **an agreed-upon statement of the school's core values**. Whose values will be taught? Who says they are important? There needs to be clear consistency between school and home on whose version of "character" will be authoritative.

In a private University-Model school, this question can be more simply answered than in a public one; but even in a public school environment it is not impossible to come to agreement on a defined set of core community values. Thomas Lickona has written a superb challenge to public educators on this subject in his article, "The Return to Character." In it, he says, "Educating for character is a moral imperative if we care about the future of our society and our children."[13]

[13] Lickona, 11.

Another excellent resource for public schools is the Character Training Institute, 520 West Main Street, Oklahoma City, OK 73102-2220. They have published a beautiful volume entitled *Achieving True Success: How to Build Character as a Family.* This resource could be made available to every family enrolled in a public University-Model school as their summary statement of shared core values. It names forty-nine qualities including attentiveness, dependability, truthfulness, orderliness, humility, and self-control. Is there a family that would not value teaching those qualities in the home?

The first school organized to test the University Model was set up as a private Christian school. Not under the sponsorship of any specific church, it adopted a statement of basic Christian doctrine (common beliefs held by most Christians) to which incoming families were asked to subscribe as part of the admissions process. This basic doctrinal statement became the basis of their agreed-upon system of core values.

Whether the core values are derived from religious faith or shared public concerns, it is imperative that the incoming families of a University-Model school be on record as sharing those values and teaching them in the home. The school makes no attempt to displace parents as the primary providers of character training. The faculty and staff do, however, make every effort to reinforce and enhance what is taught at home; but, classroom time is too short, and the scope of supervision too large (at best, 16:1) for teachers to even think of being effective in these matters if the parents are not primary.

In order to place children in the most wholesome and ordered learning environment possible, *the enrollment and hiring processes of a University-Model school asks parents and teachers alike to indicate explicit agreement with and personal commitment to the school's statement of core values.* Failure on the part of a faculty member to serve as a healthy exemplar of the school's core values can lead to questions regarding further employment.

The student enrollment process asks parents to confirm two statements in addition to their agreement with the core values. Each of these is essential in the formation of an effective character education program. First, **parents are asked to accept primary responsibility for the behavior and character development of their own children**. The school in turn agrees to encourage the students' home environments through activities aimed at strengthening family relationships and reinforcing the agreed-upon shared values. Second, since UMS students spend less time in the central classroom at school, **parents are asked to ensure the proper supervision of their own children when they are in their "satellite classrooms" at home**. Without the assurance of good parental supervision, a student's application to a UMS school may be denied.

With the agreed-upon system of core values in place, teachers can feel free to enhance the curriculum at every level with **educational materials that clarify and reinforce the core values**. This can include classroom presentations and discussions.

This leads to another necessary element in the UMS Character Development Program: **parent encouragement processes**. University-Model schools understand that their educational objectives are best served when they promote healthy home environments and loving parent-child relationships. Today's parents need encouragement, confidence, time with their children, and practical tools for some of the most important work they will ever do. Serious parents are ravenous for helps that can be offered in a spirit of support without criticism. The possible areas of focus are virtually endless. Emphasis can be given to communication among family members, managing time effectively, and strategies for discipline with love. Issues can be addressed like feelings of inferiority, peer pressure, sexual temptation, and appropriate responses to proper authority.

The methods for encouraging parents are also many. Letters of encouragement to parents highlighting commonly felt concerns can be sent. Resource libraries for parents can be made available. Seminars can be conducted that not only address key issues, but also identify resources that parents can pursue on their own. An important caution is this: parents are busy. Whatever events the school promotes to encourage parents must be "worth it," streamlining time in the most efficient way possible.

To lessen the likelihood of wasting the parents' time, it is wise not to plan seminars just for the sake of having them. It is better to have qualified, supportive people on staff who are available to assist parents as they call for specific assistance in specific situations. Over time, seminar plans can be organized around issues that have arisen out of direct experience with that school's families.

Finally, every UMS Character Education Program needs **written policies of student behavior** and **written procedures of school discipline**. Policies of behavior need to include but not necessarily be limited to matters such as order and respect in the classroom, safety and proper supervision, courtesy and consideration for others (including policies addressing racism and harassment), minimizing distractions to the learning environment, proper dress, and academic honesty. Procedures of school discipline must be defined and administered from a personal growth, not just a punishment, point of view. Instead of just rules, there need to be reasons based on the meaning of mature character. Instead of shaming, there needs to be listening for underlying causes of misbehavior so that the student can be assisted with any special needs. Instead of power wielding or anger, there needs to be steady and consistent follow-through with consequences that logically fit the offense.

Responsible parents are very supportive of straightforward, consistent policies of behavior and discipline. It is well worth the effort to have them written in clear, common-sense language.

■ Review of the Character Development Program

- An Agreed-Upon Statement of the School's Core Values
  - *Enrollment and Hiring Processes That Confirm Explicit Agreement*
- Admission Policies That Confirm Parents As Accepting

Primary Responsibility for Student Behavior at School and Student Supervision at Home
- Educational Materials That Clarify and Reinforce the Core Values
- Parent Encouragement Processes
- Written Policies of Student Behavior
- Written Procedures of School Discipline

The Student Activities Program

The Student Activities Program oversees the development of students through activities that are built around their own special interests, talents, and abilities. These include student government, sports, drama, music, art, speech, debate, and others.

The importance of the student activities program to the total development of a University-Model school should not be underestimated. The opportunity to help develop students by accessing desires, interests, aptitudes, and motivations that they already have offers untold advantages. With the students already motivated from within, involvement in these activities may be the reason some students will more naturally *want* to develop practical life skills like goal-setting and time management. As in many schools, **participation in UMS student activities is conditional upon satisfactory academic performance**. With this extra motivation to do well in all areas, students can be led to see the need for calendar planning and the maintenance of a personal schedule — disciplines that will serve them well in college as well as their future vocations.

Student activities provide opportunities for young men and women to experience the satisfaction of sacrificial effort, the dynamics of teamwork, and the bonds of friendship that are forged out of difficult tasks accomplished together. All of these contribute to the development of a student's character, leadership skills, and personal confidence.

There are also some valuable secondary benefits that come to UMS families through the student activities. First, they give parents yet one more positive point of connection with their children as they move into junior high and then high school. At a time when parents may be less involved academically, they can remain involved relationally through the natural venue of the student's positive interests. Parents can encourage their students to work hard, do their best at all times and let the rewards of achievement take their own course. Parents can be there to celebrate in the victories and give comfort in the defeats, all along affirming good character as the premium value. Student activities can provide family memories that last a lifetime.

These activities also facilitate inter-family relationships as well as provide safe, supervised family gathering places. Parents enjoy meeting other parents at these student activity events even as students enjoy meeting other students. Many times, as a part of getting acquainted, parents will begin to "compare notes" on how things are going. Often, they will gain mutual encouragement and helpful advice simply because a student activity brought the parents together informally.

The necessary elements of the Student Activities Program are similar to those of the Academic Program. First, it is necessary to have an **integrated instructional model** that properly blends the roles of professional instructor and parents in ways appropriate to the student's age. Also necessary is **professional instructors able to work in partnership with parents**, especially at the elementary level. As in the academic program, parents take a less instructional and more supportive role as students approach the older grade levels. All instructors must be positive role models, have content mastery of the activity area they teach/direct/coach, the skills to communicate that content effectively to students, and the ability to motivate and inspire students. Finally, it is necessary to have **high standards emphasizing character and a strong student work ethic**. High standards blended with a student's prior motivation to excel in a given activity make a powerful context for student character development.

Review of the Student Activities Program

- Participation in Student Activities Conditional upon Satisfactory Academic Performance
- Integrated Instructional Models
- Professional Instructors Able to Work in Partnership with Parents
- High Standards Emphasizing Character and a Strong Student Work Ethic

The Academic, Character Development, and Student Activities programs of a University-Model school work together interdependently in partnership with parents, integrating into one model the best of traditional schooling with the best of home schooling. When parents actively mentor their children in ethical and character matters, and when qualified, professional instructors are dedicated to building upon the foundation laid by those parents, then all of these programs combine to provide a dynamic preparatory environment, not only for college, but also for life.

CHAPTER 5

Parental Roles in the UMS Learning Design

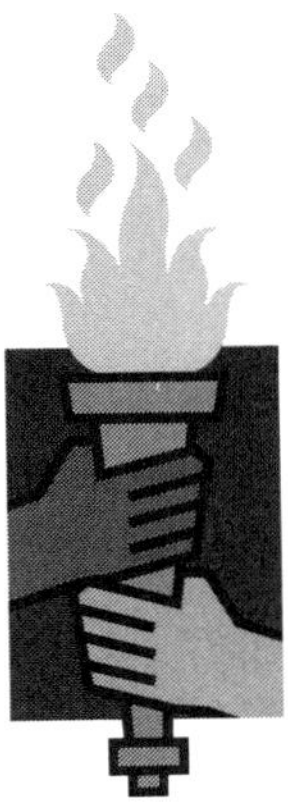

When parents and schools collaborate to help children adjust to the world of school, bridging the gap between the culture at home and the mainstream American school, children of all backgrounds tend to do well. As James Comer points out, 'children learn from people they bond to.' If children know that their parents and teachers understand and respect each other, that they share similar expectations and stay in touch, children feel comfortable with who they are and can more easily reconcile their experiences at home and school.[14]

The parent's role in a University-Model school goes far beyond simply asking children each evening, "Is your homework done?"

Academic success requires active parental mentoring, the nature of which will vary depending upon the specific course and grade level of the student. *Important to note is that the very process of being involved produces positive relational benefits that far exceed the direct benefit to the course itself.*

---

[14] Henderson, 11.

Nine different roles that parents serve in a UMS instructional model have thus far been identified. Each specific course, however, will emphasize only one of those roles as primary. Parents' understanding of and agreement to their role in each course is prerequisite to a student's acceptance in the course. In most cases, though not all, the parent's direct academic role lessens as grade levels increase. This coincides with a student's natural path toward greater independence, a process that needs to occur gradually and under parental guidance and mentoring.

There is one role *not* listed below that always applies and is compatible with each of the rest. It is the role of **Positive Motivator and Cheerleader.** Parents can experience great satisfaction and joy when they study each of their children to identify what motivates his or her best effort. With practice, they can learn how to tap those positive inner drives and passions to encourage each child toward success. Children not only need motivators, they also need cheerleaders — someone who believes in them at all times, "goes wild" when they do well, and lifts their spirits when they are down. Children never forget parents who motivate them and parents who never stop believing in them. They grow up to tell their own children about parents like that!

The nine parental roles are Primary Teacher, Co-Instructor, Private Tutor, Guide for Dependent Study, Guide for Independent Study, Course Monitor, Project Assistant, Parent Coach, and Active Supporter. Listed below are these nine parental roles and a brief description of each, beginning with the more direct roles of the earlier grades and moving toward the more supportive roles of the upper grades.

1. **Primary Teacher.** This role is usually for parents with children in first and second grade, but many parents choose to continue this role into the older grades as well. The University-Model test school offers elective classes *only* (art, physical education, etc.) for these grade levels, so that first- and second-grade students can receive their early academic instruction at home. This allows young students to have a

very positive, early education experience while they are making the gradual transition into the academic courses on campus, which can begin as early as the third grade. A University-Model school can offer workshops to these parents, assisting them as needed in the direct teaching of their children. Such workshops can eliminate some of the hours devoted to preparation and lesson planning, thus giving parents more time for the one-on-one teaching, which is usually quite simple and fun. If local and state laws are restrictive of home schooling, then a University-Model school might have to offer academic courses for first- and second-grade students as well.

2. **Co-Instructor.** Courses that use a Co-Instructor role are primarily in the elementary area, English in particular. English often encompasses more study time than any other subject in the elementary grades. As a result, responsibilities are often divided between the classroom teacher, and the parent-teacher at home. An example here is in the area of Spelling. In the UMS test school, the responsibility for spelling review is turned over completely to the parent. The classroom teacher simply provides the list and handles the testing for purposes of accountability. Little or no central classroom time, however, is used to review spelling words since it can be more effectively covered at home and one-on-one with the parent. Student character-development material blended into the curriculum in many grade levels will also actively utilize this parental role.

> *At elementary school, children whose families reinforce good work and study habits at home, emphasize the value of education, and express high expectations, tend to do well. They do even better if their parents come to school, stay informed about their progress, and collaborate with their teachers.*[15]

[15] Henderson, 18.

3. **Private Tutor.** Many elementary academic courses design this role for the parent. The courses are successful because each student has a private tutor (Mom or Dad) at home who is willing and ready to assist. Parents receive printed instructions from the classroom teacher on a regular basis outlining homework assignments, follow-up study over covered material, and preparation/review needed for the next class. Student character-development material in many grade levels will also actively utilize this parental role.

4. **Guide for Dependent Study.** This role usually applies to parents with children in grades seven through 10. Several academic courses at this level begin to cover subject matter that is unfamiliar to many parents. At the same time, the student is at a dependent age where disciplined study habits must be developed, not by parental force, but through positive encouragement and through the student's growing awareness of personal consequences. In order for the class to be successful, the teacher is dependent upon the parent to make certain that the son or daughter keeps up with the course assignments and communicates with the teacher if difficulties arise. In some cases, private tutoring by someone other than the parent may be necessary.

   The shift to middle school or junior high school is difficult for most students and their families. When parents remain involved, their children make a better adjustment, keep up the quality of their work, and develop realistic plans for their future.[16]

5. **Guide for Independent Study.** Academic courses at the eleventh- and twelfth-grade levels usually design this role for the parent. Here, parents have the opportunity to supervise the progress of their son

[16] Ibid., 18.

or daughter's independent schoolwork and provide any additional guidance they may need before entering college. Courses offered at this level will mimic that of a junior college program or higher where independent study and research skills, time management skills, a strong work ethic, and self-discipline are essential.

6. **Course Monitor.** Some courses — art, physical education, photography, foreign languages — involve equipment or expertise that require most of the teaching to be done in the classroom, leaving little for the parent at home. This role, therefore, will require the least amount of time by the parent, but its importance cannot be understated. The primary responsibility of parents is to track the progress of their students, monitoring how well they are doing. Are the students becoming discouraged? Are they enjoying the class? Do they see value in their assignments? What are the activities being done each day in class? What are they learning? In short, parents need to show an interest and express this to their children. If problems develop, students can be led to notify the teacher much sooner than they may have done on their own.

7. **Project Assistant.** With projects, parental mentoring is needed on a more intermittent basis. This role is in many respects similar to that of the Course Monitor; however, at one or more times during the semester, help at home might be needed in support of a particular project. Drama courses, for example, might involve additional help for student costuming, making puppets, working on sets, etc.

> *The few studies that look at parent involvement at the high school level reached similar findings. Students whose parents monitored their schoolwork and daily activities, talked frequently to their teachers, and helped develop their plans for*

education or work after school, were much more likely to graduate and go on to post-secondary education.[17]

8. **Parent Coach.** The role of the Parent Coach is to provide at-home, individual practice and instruction for students who are involved in athletics and/or the arts (drama, choir, band). The head coach or director will organize the overall activity, lead group practices, and communicate with parent-coaches the information and directions they will need for conducting home practices on individual skills. This role is used primarily with student athletes and artists in grades one through eight and, in some cases, grades nine and ten as well. A very pleasant benefit of this role, of course, is the privilege of attending games and performances.

9. **The Active Supporter.** This role by the parent most often relates with high school athletics and fine arts. In competitive high school student activities, the required level of training and skill needed for the activity tends to go beyond the expertise of most parents. As a result, parents are instead asked to continue mentoring their children in character matters (humility, integrity, loyalty, initiative, diligence, sportsmanship, etc.) and to actively support their children through regular attendance at games, performances, and even at practices. Parents are also encouraged to show their support by participating in organizations like booster clubs, which play vital roles in the reality of high school student activity programs. At a time when older students are beginning to increase their time away from home as they move toward independence, high school activities offer parents a regular avenue through which to remain active in their children's lives and interests.

[17] Ibid., 18.

In the published school catalogue of classes that lists each course offered by a University-Model school, there are three main sections in each printed course summary: the course description, the *parent role*, and the course prerequisites. In the parent role section, *one* of the above nine roles will be named as primary for the success of the course. By virtue of enrolling children in a class, therefore, parents agree to fulfill their respective required roles. Samples of catalogue listings are below.

6th Grade English

EE601: First Semester

EE602: Second Semester

Course Description: The sixth-grade course in English will continue to emphasize the development of skills in the use of oral and written language for the purpose of effective communication in the various subject areas. Students will be encouraged to apply their knowledge of grammar, vocabulary, and punctuation as they refine their composition skills. Sixth-grade reading materials will be drawn from a variety of genres and topics with an emphasis on literature. Students will also be introduced to some of the fundamental concepts associated with the appreciation of literature.

Parent Role: Co-instructor: Parents will receive instructions from the classroom teacher on a regular basis outlining homework assignments, follow-up study over covered material, and preparation or review needed for their next class. They will also bear the primary responsibility for direct instruction in some aspects of the course, such as spelling, and monitoring their child's academic progress (including the timely submission of all assignments).

Course Prerequisites: Satisfactory performance on the appropriate entrance test, successful completion of the preceding course in the English sequence, or permission of the instructor.

United States History (10th Grade Social Studies)

SSUS231: First Semester

SSUS232: Second Semester

Course Description: With an emphasis on the underlying causes and issues behind historical events, this course will provide students with a survey of American history from discovery to the present. The chapters on the Civil War, for example, will go beyond the main issues of slavery and states' rights and into the other underlying factors that brought about that war. Throughout the text that is used, religion's contribution to our heritage, often minimized in secular histories, will be emphasized.

Parent Role: Guide for Dependent Study: 7th-10th grade students are at a dependent age where disciplined study habits must be developed through positive encouragement and through the students' growing awareness of personal consequences. In order for these classes to be successful the teacher is dependent upon the parent to make certain that the son or daughter keeps up with the course material assigned and to communicate to the teacher if difficulties should arise. In some cases, private tutoring might even be necessary.

Course Prerequisites: Sophomore or higher classification and satisfactory performance on the appropriate entrance test or the permission of the instructor.

Physics (12th Grade Honors Science)

SCPH431: First Semester

SCPH432: Second Semester

Course Description: This course utilizes an incremental approach to the study of basic physics. Specifically, it treats the essential concepts of physics, including the basic laws of motion, statics, dynamics, work and energy, thermodynamics, optics, wave mechanics, electricity and magnetism, electrical circuits, and sub-atomic physics.

Parent Role: Guide to Independent Study: Here the parents have the opportunity to monitor the independent school work performed by their children while it is still possible for them to provide additional guidance if needed. Courses offered at this level mimic that of a Jr. College program where independent study skills and disciplined planning for completing homework assignments are necessary.

Course Prerequisites: Satisfactory performance on the appropriate entrance test and successful completion of Algebra 2 and Physical Science (or, for the second semester, the first semester of Physics) or the permission of the instructor.

CHAPTER 6

Adjusting as a Family to the University Model

Our son felt lost in the public high school he attended last year and we were worried about him getting into the wrong crowd. But he came home the other day and said, 'You know, Mom, that new school is like a close family. I really like it, but . . . man, it's hard!' That's when we knew we had made the right decision.

For years, our son attended another private school in the city. It was a good school, but by the time he was in high school, we hardly ever got to see him. University-Model Schooling gave me an opportunity to reconnect with my son. Now, every Tuesday morning, before he does his studies, he and I have a standing appointment for some father/son time. I've seen changes in both him and me already.

As much as I loved the home schooling of our four children, I have to admit that it was an overwhelming experience for me. University-Model Schooling gave me the opportunity to stay directly involved with our children without burning out. What a relief!

University-Model Schooling is different from home schooling even though it is built upon many principles and values that home-schooling parents share. Likewise,

UMS is different from traditional classroom schooling, public or private, even though it implements many dynamics and disciplines that classroom teachers employ. By trying to combine the benefits of home schooling with those of classroom teaching, UMS produces its own unique culture and standards to which incoming families must adjust. The kinds of adjustments needed vary, depending upon the family's previous experience. This chapter explores some of the adjustments that have been identified by those who have experienced the model.

Adjustments for traditional schooling families to anticipate

For families who come from a traditional classroom education experience, whether public or private, the primary adjustments to UMS can be summed up in one phrase: *more parental mentoring required.*

The word *mentoring* has been carefully chosen over the word *involvement.* "Parental involvement" is a phrase often used to describe a variety of services that parents can perform to support *school activities* in non-educational ways. The phrase "parental mentoring" is chosen to specify the actions that parents can do to direct and guide *their children* educationally.

William R. Mattox Jr. said:

> In many places today, 'parental involvement' is defined as little more than making brownies for school bake sales, being room mothers for class parties, volunteering to chaperone school field trips, serving on school advisory committees, and attending open houses, PTA meetings, sporting events, plays, and musical performances.
>
> While no one would dispute the legitimacy of some — if not all — of these functions, it is instructive that most of these traditional parental functions do not center around learning. Indeed, traditional definitions of 'parental involvement' do not fully appreciate the instructional contribution parents can and should make to their children's cognitive development.[18]

[18] William R. Mattox Jr., "The One-House Schoolroom: The Extraordinary Influence of Family Life on Student Learning," (*Family Policy*, Vol. 8, No. 4, September 1995), 4-5.

Parental mentoring — directing and guiding one's children educationally — can range all the way from providing the right environment for learning in the home to hands-on teaching and instruction. Henderson and Berla noted that children learn best when parents:

- establish a daily family routine (including regular bedtimes and times to study);
- monitor out-of-school activities (particularly television viewing);
- model the value of learning, self-discipline and hard work (especially through use of newspapers, encyclopedias, and other home educational tools);
- express high but realistic expectations for achievement (and reward success with special recognition);
- encourage children's development and progress in school (by helping with homework, maintaining dialogue with teachers, and the like);
- stimulate reading, writing, and discussions among family members (including mealtime discussions, bedtime stories and letters to relatives); and
- facilitate use of community resources (such as libraries, museums, sports programs, music lessons and cultural events).[19]

All of the above actions can sound so basic that parents may tend to underestimate the huge difference they actually make in student academic performance. Most of the time, good parental mentoring is more a function of simple alertness and everyday assertiveness than it is a matter of sophisticated or "expert" training. Even so, it is surprising how many parents fail to pay adequate attention to these foundational concerns. Such failure robs children of their best opportunity to succeed.

In UMS, parental mentoring can no longer be a mere intention or a

[19] Henderson, 9-10.

desirable "option." By virtue of the parent's agreement with the school, mentoring must become a systematic plan of action and an urgent necessity. Entering UMS moves parental mentoring to a front-and-center, word-of-honor place of priority and commitment. It is assumed that new UMS families are happy to become purposefully accountable for something that, in their deepest hearts, they already want to do.

The degree of adjustment that parents may need to this new reality can vary. Some have been actively involved in mentoring their children all along and some have not. Some have taken the time to find out from their children how things are really going in school while others have intervened only when absolutely necessary. Some have dropped the children off at school and gone off to pursue their own interests, leaving "education" to the paid professionals. Other parents have consistently searched for creative ways to stay meaningfully engaged in educating their children precisely because they are now "in school" and need wise guidance.

Parents who have had their children in traditional schools can be attracted to UMS for a number of reasons. They may like the more effective student-teacher ratio and the positive system of classroom control. They may like the higher academic standards or the college-simulated preparatory environment. They may meet other students who are attending a University-Model school and become impressed with their manners and work ethic; or, they may be hunting more available time with their children in order to stay close and keep imparting heart matters, like their faith and values. They also may desire a learning environment for their children with more explicit emphasis on the beliefs and character qualities they are teaching their children.

Whatever the reason for being attracted, it is critically important for parents to understand that the entire UMS system is organized around the foundational premise that *meaningful and positive parental mentoring makes the biggest difference in a child's education.* Good and qualified teachers are a "must." Proper administration is essential. Without parents who mentor, however, the school's methodology is unworkable, and its mission is doomed. It is imperative, therefore, that all incoming families make whatever adjustments necessary to assure a productive learning environment at home and loving family relationships. This is why the school invests in personnel and systems that encourage families, as they need it, through this critical component of their transition to UMS.

One UMS parent has observed, "If you dreaded the day that you had to send your kids off to first grade because you were going to miss them so much, then UMS may be for you. But if you could not wait to put your children in school so that you could get them out of your hair, then UMS is not what you are looking for."

■ Adjustments for home-schooling families to anticipate

Home-schooling parents are the ones who know best that not all home-schooling families are alike. They are, in fact, quite diverse in their reasons for home schooling, their methods of tailoring instruction for their children, and their patterns of interaction with the larger community. Parents can be motivated to home school by a blended variety of spiritual, relational, educational, and social considerations. One family's deepest motivation may be spiritual, desiring maximum together-time for living out their faith and passing it along to the next generation. Another's deepest influencing factor may be relational, wanting to become and remain a close-knit and caring family. Still another may focus most on educational factors, preferring individualized, tutorial instruction to the more generalized classroom approach. Finally, others may be most motivated by social factors, desiring to shield children as much as possible from any number of potentially destructive societal influences like drugs, violence, or world views that contradict the family's basic beliefs and values.

It is possible, of course, for a family to be motivated to some degree by all of the above factors, while one of them remains primary. It is also possible for a family to be so motivated by one factor that the others pale in comparison. A home-schooling family strongly motivated by spiritual factors may also be highly involved in meaningful relationships and service outside the home, while another, motivated mostly by social factors and concerns, may be highly reclusive. Because the particular combination of motivational factors and the importance placed on each can vary so much from family to family, it is difficult to predict the exact adjustments to UMS needed in each case; nevertheless, two general issues of adjustment have been identified as common for those coming from a home-schooling experience: *fewer controllable factors* and *more activity options.*

The first issue of adjustment is *fewer controllable factors.* Home-schooling parents who have enjoyed maximum, individualized control over a child's learning process, schedule, curriculum, and pace must share in a new partnership with the UMS calendar and curriculum. While there are many benefits in the partnership, there are also some felt losses. Cooperation translates into accepting a more generalized structure, complete with firmer deadlines. Most home-schooling parents who enter UMS readily comprehend and accept the need for this cooperation, but it still takes a period of time to adjust to a system that has less individual autonomy and mobility than that provided by pure home schooling.

What is not lost, however, is the acceptance and support of parents as the primary educators of their children. One long-time home-schooling parent commented, "The reason why we enrolled our high-school-aged children in this school was because it was the first time we had sensed sincere support from school officials for what we had been doing with our children up until that time. Enrolling our children then was not a change in our philosophy, but a continuation of it." It follows that this parent found the process of adjusting to fewer controllable factors an acceptable one because she remained in an environment that explicitly encouraged and affirmed the kind of active involvement that she wished to maintain with her high school students.

Another area in which home-schooling parents encounter the issue of fewer controllable factors is in the number of friendship influences that can push and pull on their children's beliefs and values. Even when every family enrolled has endorsed the agreed-upon system of core school values, individual differences and human nature make a certain level of conflict inevitable. Frankly, some parents adjust to this reality by returning to the safety of the pure home-schooling environment they once enjoyed. Most parents, however, use these conflicts as opportunities to further guide their children in character-development matters like standing for what is right even when it is unpopular and learning to love and sincerely appreciate those who disagree. Once again, the key to a good result is alert and active parental mentoring, which is specifically promoted and endorsed by the University-Model Schooling community.

The second issue of adjustment for home-schooling families is *more activity options*. For some families, this is welcome. For others, it is a crisis. In pure home schooling, Mom and Dad have the luxury of carefully selecting the list of possible outside-the-home activities, saying "no" to many before the kids even hear about them. In UMS, Mom and Dad still choose, of course, but the list of possible activities begins to grow. Children hear about opportunities at school — everything from birthday parties to sleep-overs to school sporting events to after-the-game get-togethers to bowling nights to movies in a home or theater. Parents who rightly value the need to properly investigate and supervise their children's activities can feel a great deal more pressure in decision-making than they did before. While the kids are urgently insisting that "everyone" is going, wise parents must take the time to gather the pertinent facts from the proper supervising adult, then have the courage to respectfully decline the opportunity if it seems necessary to do so. This intensified need for managing the children's informal social life can be a stressful adjustment for many parents.

The good news, however, is that the adjustment to more activity options can be gradual and not necessarily all-at-once. Many home-schooling parents enroll their children in only one to three classes the first year. This gives them an opportunity to experience the UMS system and identify their own transition strategy. It also gives them time to get valuable practice in coordinating the social dynamics of a larger school setting. Some parents decide after the first year to transition their students toward a full load of classes while others prefer to continue taking only a few classes to supplement the primary curriculum at home. The beauty of UMS is that parents have the freedom to determine the level of involvement that best suits them.

Summary

Home-schooling parents, already accustomed to a high level of involvement with their children, generally need to adjust to (1) fewer controllable factors and (2) more activity options as they enter into partnership with a University-Model School. Traditional schooling parents, already accustomed to a high level of activity for their children, generally need to adjust to the increased obligation to mentor their children — spiritually, academically, and socially — as they enter into partnership with UMS. The happy balance between healthy parental involvement and wholesome, quality activities is one of the attractions that many families feel to UMS.

CHAPTER 7

Frequently Asked Questions About UMS

Did my UMS high school get me ready for college? Let me put it this way: high school was harder! I'm making all A's in college right now.

I guess I first began to realize how prepared I was when my freshman English teacher in college assigned a five-page research paper. You wouldn't believe how many guys around me started to panic. And I'm like, "Are you kidd'n?!" I remember doing ten- to fifteen-page papers in English AND History when I was a high school JUNIOR. Yeah, you can go tell everybody — I was ready for college!

When I got to college, I saw a lot of guys get out of class then just go out and goof off. They weren't used to doing homework or planning their time outside of class — they never had to in high school. Some of them had to flunk a course or two before they woke up. I feel like I never missed a beat. College was just like going to a UMS high school, only not quite as hectic.

Are colleges accepting students from the University-Model test school? What makes them attractive to colleges over other students?
Students from the UMS test school have had no difficulty in gaining entrance

to colleges and universities nationwide. In fact, the majority of graduates have been awarded scholarships for academic achievement, student leadership, and athletic or artistic ability. The UMS test school stays informed on the current and projected entrance requirements of the major four-year universities. This allows school officials to be sure that the course offerings are meeting or exceeding college standards. In addition, UMS test-school students are attractive to colleges because of their strong work ethic, successful study habits, leadership skills, and character as demonstrated through various student activities — academic, athletic, artistic, and governmental.

How are UMS students doing on college entrance tests?

Despite admission policies aimed at average students, the UMS test-school students score much higher on college entrance tests than the average scores nationwide. At the time of this writing, 10 percent of the test school's senior class of 2001 qualified as national merit scholars during their junior years. (Less than 1 percent of all students nationwide score this well.) As seniors, this same class is expected to meet the test school's target average of 1,200 on their college SAT entrance scores. (Average scores nationwide are approximately 1,000.)

My wife and I both work full time outside our home. Would UMS work for us?

One of the most important ingredients in the success of the University Model is an available parent who can assist and properly work with the student. For a family in which both parents work outside the home on a full-time basis, a more traditional 35-40 hours/week school is probably the better choice. Exceptions to this might be made in the cases of some older high school students who have previously demonstrated an acceptable level of maturity and self-discipline. Even then, regular and proper accountability would be important. As a general rule, improper supervision of children and youth creates the possibility of too many counterproductive situations.

I have children in several different grade levels. How much time will each need to spend doing schoolwork on their days at home?
The rule of thumb at the UMS test school is that for every hour spent in class at school, the student will need to spend an additional hour on that subject in the "satellite classroom" at home. This rule, of course, varies according to the need. If a student is academically strong in a particular area, perhaps less time will be needed. If a student is weak in a subject or the subject is particularly challenging, then more time will be needed. Also, eleventh and twelfth graders may average more than an hour studying for each hour in class since the material is more advanced. Parents need to be alert to each of their children's individual needs and lead them accordingly in the structuring of their time.

Since parents are team teaching with the teachers at school, how does communication take place between the two?
Communication between teachers and parents plays a large role in a UMS test school, and there are several ways that clear communication can take place. First, each course is described, along with its prerequisite and parent role, in the school catalogue. The parent role is defined for each course so that parents understand the required level of assistance for their children. Also, on the first day of class each semester, instructors provide take-home lists that describe how grades are determined, what supplies will be needed, and the general course outline. Vitally important next are the printed weekly assignment sheets that are prepared by the teacher to be taken home and reviewed by the parent with the student. Instructions to parents are included as part of these assignment sheets as are long-term study projects that are forthcoming, like research papers. Parents are also invited to communicate any of their questions back to the teacher as needed.

What about peer pressure? Is it as strong in UMS as it seems to be in traditional schools?
Many students who enter the University-Model test school from traditional schools indicate that, by comparison, the peer pressure is more

positive than it was in their previous school. In other words, the peer culture of a University-Model school tends to apply stronger than average "pressure" toward doing the right things — showing respect, being honest, working hard, doing one's best, and so forth. This can be attributed to the students themselves, the UMS system of support for parental values through the character education program, and the students' stronger than average relationships with their parents due to having more time together as provided by the program design.

What is the difference between home-school co-ops and University-Model schools?

UMS and home-school co-ops should not be equated. Home-school co-ops are a good way for home-schooling families to pool their resources and expertise for specific and usually short-term study projects. One parent, for instance, may be especially proficient in math or science and teach a group of students that subject for a period of time. Generally speaking, home-school co-ops are age-integrated, specialized, parent-run, and do not simulate a college structure. In some cases, co-ops also take over the primary responsibility of teaching certain courses instead of integrating the teacher and parent effectively for each course as is done in the University Model. UMS is also different by virtue of having specific grade levels, consistent accountability from semester to semester, a full spectrum of courses complete with prerequisites and diploma plans, and a professional administration and faculty (much like a traditional school would have) partnering with the parents.

My child is gifted in math and science, but English gives him trouble. How can UMS help him?

The UMS test school allows a student to advance by course mastery, not age or grade level alone. Elementary students are allowed to move up or down one grade level in a given course subject. Junior high and high school students may advance up two grade levels or move back two. For instance, a nine-year-old student (normally a fourth-grader) may be placed in a fifth-grade English class (up one level) and a third-grade math class (down one level) in the same year if his aptitudes and needs warrant. This is quite acceptable and common in the UMS test school where advancement is by individual course and not by a whole grade level.

How does the cost differ between full-time traditional private schools and University-Model schools?
Present tracking of existing models indicates that University-Model private schools should be 25 to 50 percent less in cost than the average traditional private school.

We cannot afford any type of private school. How feasible are University-Model public schools?
We would like to believe that University-Model public schools are very feasible in light of the U.S. Department of Education's stated priorities of getting families more involved in education, reducing class size, improving academic achievement (especially reading and math), and strengthening school construction. Public University-Model charter schools, serving alongside traditional public schools, would offer communities an increased possibility of meeting all these objectives. A UMS school can take a facility that normally serves 600 students and utilize it for serving either 1,000 students with the same student/teacher ratio or the same 600 students with a drastically improved student/teacher ratio. Either way, this can save states money in building construction and/or personnel costs. The cost savings gained by such schools can be applied to meet additional educational needs. For instance, each year's per-student savings could be donated to a college fund for UMS students who come from financially disadvantaged families. The net expense to the state would be the same, while more could be done with each dollar.

What do your graduates who are in college say about how well-prepared they were in high school?

Graduates from the University-Model test school report overwhelmingly that they were extremely well-prepared for their freshman college classes. (See quotes at the beginning of this chapter.) First, they were prepared by the University-Model system itself. The schedule, work ethic, and necessary study skills were dynamics to which they were already accustomed. Second, they were prepared academically. The UMS course content was consistently more than adequate to get students ready for college. It also has not been uncommon for many UMS graduates to begin college with several college credits already on their transcript, having placed out of certain courses by virtue of their high school preparation.

WOULD YOU LIKE MORE INFORMATION?

GPA Ministries is a non-profit organization established for the purpose of developing, improving, and promoting University-Model Schooling nationwide for students in grades 1-12.

GPA Ministries publishes a monthly newsletter that contains updated information about University-Model schools in your area, information about seminars on How to Start a University-Model school, and other helpful information.

You may *receive a free sample* of our monthly newsletter or *subscribe* by writing:

GPA Ministries
P. O. Box 60154
Fort Worth, Texas 76115

A suggested annual donation of $25 would be greatly appreciated to cover the publishing and mailing costs of your newsletter subscription.